GAINING THE **VICTORY** OVER YOUR **THOUGHT** LIFE

VOLUME 1

**Gaining the Victory Over Your Thought Life
Volume I**
Copyright © 2015
Author Terrance Cheatham
Cover design: Anointed Fire™ House
Publisher: Anointed Fire™ House
Publisher's Website: www.anointedfirehouse.com

*All scriptures noted in this book were taken from the
King James bible unless otherwise noted.*

ISBN-13: 978-0692543863

ISBN-10: 0692543864

Dedications

- *First and foremost, I want to express my sincerest gratitude to my Heavenly Father for redeeming, teaching, trusting, loving and investing in me. He has led and guided me through my own process of truly learning and discovering that authentic victory is the intangible experience that happens on the inside of us before it ever gets to a stage to be lived out on the outside of us... I love you Father.*

- *To my dear wife... for the occasional, "How is that book coming?" You kept pushing and holding me accountable through times of stagnation and distraction. Thank you, sweetie, for believing in what God has said and spoken over my life throughout the years... I love you.*

- *To my adorable children for remaining consistent, keeping me balanced and understanding my call. Thank you for the laughter, jokes and all the smiles that make every day worthwhile... Daddy loves you.*

- *To Sufficient Grace Christian Center and all those who have made significant contributions to my journey... without your touch this wouldn't be possible... Thank you, thank you and thank you again.*

Table of Contents

Introduction

In spite of the vast strides we have made in technology, along with the marriage between science and medicinal research, mankind has not yet been able to understand but a small minuscule of how the human brain works and what it is capable of. What we can all agree on is the fact that our brains, which house our thoughts are the most complex but least understood organs in our bodies. Fret not, in this book my desire is not to try to delve into the complexities that are often associated with navigating the anatomy of the brain, but rather, to explore what we can do and employ strategies that we can apply to winning the ever elusive victory over our inner life, also known as our "thought life."

Many people have made an unconscious covenant with dysfunctional thought patterns, because after all, "dysfunction" is still "functional" to some degree. Over time, it becomes very possible to function within our abnormal thinking for so long that "abnormal" dresses itself up in "normal" clothes. When this happens, we will no longer see the need for thought renovation, let alone, any real reason as to why we should change our thought life. Even as you read this introduction, you have already envisioned the faces of people you believe could stand to read this book or perhaps fit the mold of what I have already described. Out of all the faces you saw, how many of those faces were YOURS? Don't feel bad. It is our "normal" human proclivity to turn our attention outward (closely examining others that we think need to be fixed), but please remember that as you look OUT, your attention has been drawn away from what is happening IN you. In this book, you will learn how to systematically gain the victory over your thought life; not everyone else's, but YOURS! This book has the potential to shift the next chapter of your life, so take a deep breath and exhale. Let's take this journey together!

CHAPTER 1
Renovation Of The Mind

"Renovation: to make changes and repairs to (an old house, building, room, etc.) with the intentions of restoring it to its original condition." www.merriam-webster.com/dictionary/renovation

Merriam-Webster describes the word renovation as: the undertaking of a project that needs to be restored because it has become outdated or perhaps no longer efficient in serving relevant needs. In most cases, when the word renovation is mentioned, we are typically binary in our thinking. Renovation has to pertain either to a house or a building, but very seldom do we consider that periodically our thinking has to undergo the same renovation process that a physical structure has to undergo. It is true that our minds are a different type of edifice, but it is an edifice nonetheless. In most cases, renovating the mind requires more sacrifices, more time, and more effort than restoring any house or building I can think of! I have seen new homes built from the ground up in as little as 9-12 months, and on the flip side of that coin, I have seen people take 9-12 years (if not more) to even begin entertaining the idea that their minds *might* need make-overs.

Nobody goes through the tedious and painstaking task of renovating anything, without first being fully persuaded that what they are renovating is no longer profitable in the current state that it is in. I remember the first church my wife and I had the privilege of planting. It was an abandoned and modest beauty salon located in a small town, but it had the *potential* of meeting all our needs at the time. There was only one thing that stood in our way. Before it could be what we needed it to be, it had to be renovated. *Wait a minute!* Renovation meant lots of hard work, money and resources we did not have, and oh yeah, did I mention lots of hard work?

What I have learned to love about renovations is the fact that anyone who dares to take on the task of renovating something, only does so because they see the potential of what they are about to renovate! They see something in the project that is worth the time, dedication, hard work, investment and ultimately, the sacrifice. Eventually the sacrifice will pay greater dividends than the effort required for the renovation itself. Just like my first church building, your mind has everything it needs to serve and aid you in living out your God-given purpose to the optimum capacity, but YOU have to FIRST see that your mind and thought process, in its *current state,* does not have the capacity to produce the end result that you desire. As it was with that old, small and abandoned hair salon, you must entertain the possibility that the only thing standing between your potential and you actualizing that potential is YOUR thought process.

<u>YOU</u> Have To See It First!

There's something I learned several years ago as I found myself bumping into the same wall, at the same place, at the same time and in the same way... *you get the point*. A very influential mentor in my life at that time kept bringing the "wall" that I had a proclivity for banging my head into to my attention. The more my mentor would bring it up, the more determined I became to not hit the wall. To my dismay, I realized that I had stopped running into the "wall", but the problem was, I was only able

to avoid it if my mentor warned me that I
was headed towards it!

You see, the "wall" was MY problem,
not my mentor's problem, and it did not
profit me to avoid the crash based upon his
observation of it. **I HAD TO SEE THE WALL
FOR MYSELF** if I was going to avoid it
without someone else bringing it to my
attention. I discovered that without
personal discernment and awareness of <u>self</u>,
we have the tendency to fix our brokenness
during the short seasons, when someone
else is present to identify what is broken in
our lives. Once those seasons are over and
their observations cease, our repair of self
ceases. Why is this? Because, in our own
eyes, we didn't have the problems they said
needed to be fixed in the first place.
Beloved, YOU have to see your thought
patterns as a problem before you will or can
renovate them. We, as human beings, have
the tendency to believe that whatever we

think about something is not only our
truth, but THE TRUTH, THE WHOLE TRUTH,
AND NOTHING BUT THE TRUTH! To unlearn
misconceptions developed within our mind
is and can be one of the most difficult things
to do. In part, it is that way because so
many different people, events and
situations aided in the contribution of those
beliefs.

We have to come to a day of
reckoning within ourselves, where we are
passionate enough about experiencing the
highest expression of who God created us
to be that we do not shy away from
personal interrogation. We must take the
keys God has given us and unlock the
stranger within. This way, we can truly
become free of old adages that have been
so ingrained within our thinking that we
hold many of them to be truths, when in
fact, many of them are bold-faced lies!
Have you ever heard the adage, "If it ain't

broke, don't fix it?"(Excuse my poor vernacular). Most of us have; in fact, many of you reading this have probably quoted it, or at least, thought about it and presumably bought into the principle of it. This idea in a nutshell is: "Leave well enough alone." But what if "well enough" no longer serves you as it once did in the past?

I have discovered that in most instances, people are not willing to fix what is in fact, **very broken**, mainly because they would much rather adjust their lives to fit within the context of what is broken. Beloved, you must remember that dysfunctional is still functional! The blessing and curse of being so fearfully and wonderfully made by our Creator is the fact that no matter what environment you place us in, whether good or bad, if you leave us in it long enough, we will adapt and adjust to it. Unfortunately, anything you abide in long enough becomes normal (to you) after a while, even if it is an abnormal condition. To be truly healed in your thinking requires a great deal of humility, because the process demands that you are able to collect the evidence, look at all the clues, and declare your own mind guilty of treason! The truth is you will never take affirmative action against your thought life until you realize that YOUR MIND HAS BETRAYED YOU!!!

CHAPTER 2
It's Time To Upgrade Your Software!

Interestingly, the Bible speaks frequently about "renewing the mind", and if you own a cell phone, computer, or any other high speed gadget (I can't keep up with all the names or types), you probably understand why. I am not a technology guru by a long shot, but I am smart enough to surround myself with people who are. Not long ago, my wife and I began to experience issues with our desktop computer. It was moving very slowly (almost not at all). When we decided to bring in the Calvary and fight an all-out battle with our computer, an acquaintance of mine who ironically owns a computer repair shop came by my place of business and struck up a casual conversation with me. I began to inform him of my computer's unwillingness to comply with my demands, and after listening to me belittle my computer (that was not present to defend itself, by the way), he asked me one simple question: "Have you been accepting the upgrades?" Almost offended, I confidently replied, "No way; those things are dangerous and may contain viruses." My friend's eyes grew wide as he began to explain the real problem. He began to explain to me (as a seasoned teacher would expound to his disciple), "Your problem is that you are not receiving the upgrades." He went on to say, "**The upgrades actually prevent viruses and contain cures for glitches in outdated software**."

Just like my computer, when we refuse to upgrade or renew our minds, we make ourselves vulnerable to glitches and cycles of thinking that are no longer profitable for us to operate in. As I previously stated, we tend to try to avoid bad outcomes by avoiding better ways of getting better outcomes. My biggest problem was that I didn't know enough about the advantages of new upgrades to let go of the outdated software! I am a firm believer that as born again Kingdom people, we must develop a relationship with the Word of God. That's because nestled deep down in the Holy Scriptures are the guidelines that teach us how to live, function, operate and how we ought to think in this new Kingdom we have been born into. I have had the privilege of serving in ministry for close to 15 years, and within that time, I have pastored three churches (internationally and domestically)... two of which my wife and I planted. I have heard many sincere and kindhearted believers tell me time and time again how difficult it is for them to serve God. I have discovered that it is not hard to serve God; the challenge is giving yourself permission to become compatible with the Kingdom God birthed you into.

God births us into His Kingdom when we are born again, but it is our choice to accept or not accept the upgrades of that Kingdom provided to us by the Holy Spirit. The Bible clearly tells us that the renewal of our thinking is our personal responsibilities. In other words, YOU will be changed at the rate in which your thinking changes. If you are not putting new information in, you cannot expect new results to come out. Over the years, I have observed many people become increasingly frustrated with their own church attendance because the preacher's sermons often represented a life of victory that they felt they had no chance of experiencing on a personal level.

Mental defeat is the worst kind because in most cases, nobody knows another person's dilemma except that person. The reason for this is that many struggle secretly with the burden of living up to a standard in public that they cannot make work for them in private. Yes, these frustrated individuals volunteer at church, shout during praise and worship, work hospitality with a smile, and even "amen" the preacher when he or she hits certain points. Nevertheless, they never recognize that every portion of the service was designed to offer "upgrades" to the outdated software of their thinking. Because of this, they leave a high moment at church to live a low life in private because the "upgrade" was denied, and in many cases, not even recognized. An individual can become so locked into an antiquated way of thinking that the offer of thinking differently will not register or seem like a possibility to them. **WINNING THE BATTLE AT CHURCH DOESN'T MEAN YOU WON THE BATTLE IN YOUR HEAD!** If you are the person being described, you are likely ready

to renovate, renew and restore your mind…
let's get to work!

CHAPTER 3
Off With Your Head!

In medieval times, the presiding authority over an execution would yell to the Headsmen (person carrying out the task), "Off with their head!" With one swift, clean stroke of the blade, the victim's head would be removed from his or her body with surgical precision. It was a clean and sure death, since everything that regulates the function of the body lies within the head. Get the head and everything else will follow! If they could take a person's head, they could take that person's life or better yet, gain control of everything that person had control of. Depending on the scenario, the decapitated heads would be placed on staffs at the entrance of a city or some other conspicuous location. The severed heads were used to warn criminals, traitors or opposing nations, and in some cases, they were considered trophies. It was a sign of dominance by the person, if I may say, on the "better end" of the sword. We are in a spiritual war that often manifests its destruction in the natural areas of our lives. You don't hear the gunfire, rocket propelled grenades, or the fighter jets zooming overhead, but you do see the evidence of the attacks in your life. Just as in medieval times, the enemy is coming for your head because if he can take your head, he gains control of everything else in your life.

You must understand why your head is so important. As a child, I used to often scurry up to my uncle's house to eat hot dogs and watch my favorite childhood drama, Tom and Jerry (be kind, it was a drama to me). Now that I'm older, I don't know whether I was more desirous of the cartoons or to see my uncle's diverse collection of wall mounts from the many different animals he had hunted. I can recall asking him on one occasion why he had the heads of these animals mounted on his wall, and his response was, "It reminds me of the hunt." What I am attempting to convey is the fact that "hunters" love to keep the "heads" of what they have conquered! The Bible describes Satan as one who hunts in 1 Peter 5:8. The scripture says it this way, "Be alert and sober minded. Your enemy the devil prowls around like a roaring lion looking for someone to devour" (NIV translation). Yes, your enemy, the devil, is hunting you and will try his best to keep your "head" in his possession!

The enemy knows that if he can behead you, he can control everything else that pertains to your life. In Proverbs 23:7, the Bible teaches us that a person is the byproduct of their thought life, so in essence, if the enemy is able to take your head captive, you become a slave to him. It deeply saddens me to even imagine how many born again believers are mentally enslaved to what I like to call "can't help it". Unfortunately, many of us can relate to the proverbial, "I just can't stop

_____," **(fill in the blank).** At some point, we have all struggled with something. Honestly, many of us still struggle with certain things (post salvation) that we secretly believe are indestructible. When you were filling out the blank above, did you happen to notice the level of integrity and transparency that is required to truly interrogate yourself without making an excuse, churchifying it, or justifying what you have become a slave to mentally? The price of getting free mentally is expensive because it requires you to be transparent with yourself.

Too many people are enslaved to the lives their own mental reasoning has created for them! Consider this: It is recorded in the fifth chapter of St. John in the Bible that there was a "certain man" who, along with many other sick and disabled individuals, would gather at a pool of water in Jerusalem called Bethesda. John goes on to say, "that an angel went down at a certain season into the pool, and troubled the water: whosoever stepped into the troubled waters was made whole of whatsoever disease they had." John describes this "certain man" as having had an infirmity for 38 years! It implies that for 38 years, this man had been sick. He had also been close enough to the pool to be healed of his condition, but never received the healing that he waited for. The bible says that Jesus approached this man and asked him, "Will you be made whole?" The man replied with excuses for not being healed without ever answering the question asked of him.

Whether we realize it or not, our "infirmities" interpret excuses as justification! In other words, every time we make an excuse for our problems, we are, in fact, giving those problems permission to exist in our lives. Here is how it sounds: "I'm like this because_____"**(fill in the blank).** When we talk like that, we are giving the infirmity a reason to be in our lives. When we are in a bad condition (even mentally) for long periods of time, a better condition is no longer an option, even though we gather around the pool with all the other sick folk *waiting* on something better to happen. I need you to dig deep and honestly right here, because our minds have taught us to pray, quote scriptures, and wait on changes to come that we no longer expect to happen! This "certain man", at one time in his life, wanted to be made whole, but over time, his own mind had made allowances for him to remain in the condition he was in until what once was an abnormal condition had now become a normal experience for him. How many of us can draw a connection between ourselves and this "certain man" who had a condition that became more important than his name?

REFLECTIONS

*What are some similarities between you and the "certain man"?

_____

_____

_____

_____

_____

_____

*What are some of the excuses you use to justify you not being made whole?

_____

_____

_____

_____

_____

_____

*Can you identify some of the "sick folk" around you who make abnormal appear normal?

_____

_____

_____

_____

_____

_____

*What steps can you take NOW to move
beyond what your mind has made
allowances for?

_____

_____

_____

_____

_____

_____

*What will you do to be more transparent
with yourself?

_____

_____

_____

_____

_____

_____

CHAPTER 4

If You Don't Understand The War, How Can You Win The Battle?

The Bible tells us how we've been enlisted into a war we didn't exactly sign up for. In the Apostle Paul's letter to the Roman church, he explained the source of the "civil war" that often takes place within believers (read Roman 1:21-23). He goes on in verse 25 to reveal something very interesting. Apostle Paul says, "With the *mind* I serve the law of God." Now, armed with this information, if you were the devil, where would you yield your greatest attack if you wanted to disrupt a person's ability to serve God and reach their God-given purpose and potential? You would attack the mind, of course, or any other place that has the ability to draw the mind away from God and towards something else. Not

25

convinced yet? Think about the many times this very tactic (in whatever form it manifested) has sabotaged your own ability to prioritize your thinking to the point where you were not only unable to put God first but to actually KEEP God first.

At some point, we have all been victimized by the assassin of the mind because we were unaware of the fact that we had been victimized. The mind is a very powerful thing and when it has been the subject of attack for long periods of time, it becomes easy to justify the bullet wounds. A major part of the assault is not just distractions, but justification for the damage caused by the attack. You cannot defend something if you are not aware it is under attack. For example, how many times has your thinking been violated by the enemy to the point where God was no longer first, but you justified demoting Him because you believed, at that moment, something more important came up? As I stated in a previous chapter, getting free mentally will cost you the high price of transparency with self. You have to be willing to admit that you have a tendency of making adjustments to God's position in your life based upon what YOU deem to be an emergency. If you study the pattern carefully, you may discover that everything that pops up after you decide to make God first always appears to come dressed in emergency clothes. Remember, beloved, this book is designed to challenge you to explore YOU at a deeper level than you normally would so that you will be able to recognize where the enemy has found a weakness in your thinking.

All too often, we become defensive and respond with the proverbial: "I know God is first in my life!" That's our rebuttal

whenever we are challenged in regards to
God's position in our lives. I am glad that
you know He is first in your life, but does
God know He's first and would He agree
with you? Before you jump to a conclusion,
have you really examined the facts? Here
are a few things to consider:

1. When God is really first in your life,
   you will always seek Him and His things
   first; EVERYTHING else is secondary
   (see Matthew 6:33). Are you actively
   involved in a local church and
   consistently witnessing to the lost (see
   Hebrews 10:25 and Acts 1:8)? If you
   are in ministry, do you live what you
   preach and preach what you live (see
   Matthew 5:19)? When things "come
   up" to interrupt points 1 and 2, what do
   you usually sacrifice: God or the
   "distraction" that is disguised as an
   emergency? If you are struggling to

understand what these scenarios have to do with whether or not God is first in your life, my point has been proven. According to the words of Jesus recorded in the Gospel of Matthew 22: 37-40, scenarios 1 and 2 sum up the whole duties of mankind in a nutshell.

We have to come to the realization that we cannot win a war if we do not understand why we are fighting. The enemy is literally trying to take over the **head**quarters of our lives and kill us with "friendly fire." *Friendly fire* is a term used in war to describe an event where you are killed by a person or by people on your own team. I am suggesting to you, my friend, that the enemy is attempting to use YOU against YOU! In other words, your enemy can be your inner-me.

CHAPTER 5
Spiritual Warfare: Forethought or Afterthought?

2 Corinthians 10:3-5

What I have discovered is that most people do not posture themselves for the battle until they have already been made the subject of an attack. This is very dangerous, especially as it relates to the mind, because once the enemy breaches the mind, he is no longer shooting outside the gates, but is now waging war inside the **head**quarters (pun intended). This tactic reminds me of the horse decoy in the movie Troy. The Trojans ignorantly brought a giant wooden edifice shaped like a horse that they believed the Greeks had built as an offering to Poseidon, the Sun God, into their fortress. They thought the horse was a sign of victory. As the Trojans celebrated deep into the night, the Greek commandos who were lying wait inside the horse, revealed themselves and began to plunder the city from *inside* the walls. How many victories have you celebrated too soon?

If the REAL battle is waged *inside* the **head**quarters, there must be soldiers able to fight the enemy *inside* the gates! Let me explain. The Bible instructs us to bring "every thought captive to the knowledge of God (see 2 Corinthians 10:5)." This implies that in order to bring bad thoughts captive, you must have some Word in your head to capture it with or compare it to. How do we do this? Every bad thought must be replaced with a better thought that provides a better promise. To overthrow bad thoughts, we have to capture and then replace those thoughts with scriptures that promise us a better reward than the simple pleasures of bad thinking. Let's be honest; sometimes, bad thoughts can feel good.

Bad thoughts can be defined as any thought that does not line up with or goes against God's Word.

The writer made it very clear, "The weapons of our warfare are not carnal, but mighty through God to the pulling down of strongholds (2 Corinthians 10: 3-5)." There are three things that MUST happen if we are to regain control of our **head**quarters:

1. We can't keep going after decoys that provoke us to fight spirits in our flesh (our natural ability).

2. We must make sure that God recognizes the fight we are enlisting Him in.

3. When we get 1 and 2 right, strongholds (old ways of thinking) will be brought down.

Many believers are engaging in what I like to call "shadow boxing". We are snatching, scratching and swinging at things that are not really there. I made my first attempt at boxing in a small rundown boxing club when I was 11 years old. Although my boxing career lasted as long as my first visit, what the trainer taught me would last a lifetime. The trainer said to me, "Your goal is to never swing if you can't land the punch. It takes twice as much energy to swing and miss than it does to land a punch." No wonder most people in church are always so tired and worn out. They have been fighting ghosts all week!

We have to be sure we are enlisting God to help us fight a battle HE recognizes. Just because you call something the enemy does not mean that it is. We use a plethora of Christian colloquialisms that indeed sound very deep and spiritual, but many of them beg the questions: Are you swinging and missing? Does God even recognize the fight? Are you picking a fight with the right opponent? The enemy employs a tactic that many of us are totally unaware of that I like refer to as "smoke and mirrors". Sound familiar? Magicians use this technique to fool you into believing that something is real, when in fact, it is not. They do this by drawing your attention away from what they are really doing. As with the magician, the enemy produces decoys (lesser important things) to take your focus off the main thing (the most important thing). You must understand, when you turn your attention away from the main thing to fight a decoy, you expose yourself to greater levels of attack from the real enemy; the very enemy you should have been fighting in the first place. By the time you realize you have been duped and hoodwinked, you have swung and missed so many times that you have very little (if any) energy left to fight the real enemy and win.

Don't Bring A Knife To A Gun Fight

Have you ever heard the old adage "don't bring a knife to a gun fight?" In a nutshell, it translates to mean: *come prepared for the situation at hand*! 2 Corinthians 10:3-4 informs us that we live in this flesh, but we do not and should not engage the enemy in our flesh. One of the biggest problems we have in warfare is that we have a tendency to resort to how we used to handle things. I call it "operating on default". If you think long and hard, you will recognize a pattern that reemerges every time YOU attempt to fix your head. You approach the battle leaning on carnal things for support: television, people, Facebook, drugs, sex, alcohol, food, impulsive spending, nonproductive busyness, willpower, and every other distraction that never works long term, but in most cases, makes matters worse.

The enemy of the mind counts on us and even predicts that we will lean on our carnality (human effort/devices) to try and fight him on a spiritual landscape. When we attempt to fight a spiritual enemy in the flesh, what we are really doing is self-medicating, not realizing that the enemy uses the things we medicate with to bring us even lower. Self-medicating in whatever form, NEVER WORKS because the problem is not "out there"; the problem is "in here" (the mind). It is an inner issue that cannot be fixed by an outer source.

If our weapons are not carnal, then what are they? The NIV translation says it this way, "The weapons we fight with are not weapons of the world. On the contrary, they have divine power to demolish strongholds. We demolish arguments and every pretension that sets itself up against the knowledge of God, and we take captive every thought to make it obedient to

Christ." Now, we must understand that the application of this instruction can be very challenging to the self-medicating thought patterns that we have developed over the years. However, I believe Jesus had us in mind when He allowed us to peak into the wilderness and witness Him being tested by Satan so that we could see firsthand how this level of warfare is executed.

In the Gospel of Matthew, chapter 4 verses 1 through 4, we find Jesus being viciously assaulted in the wilderness through the suggestive power of the enemy. Jesus has just been baptized, the Holy Spirit descended upon Him as a dove, the Father has validated Him as the Son of God, and immediately, He is led by the Spirit into the wilderness to be tested without any witnesses. It is immediately after Jesus has completed a forty day fast that the enemy begins to fire off suggestions at His mind. *If you have ever fasted at least four days then you understand exactly what I am talking about.*

Jesus was in a place where not only did He become vulnerable and weakened, but His mind also became active. The Bible says that Jesus was hungry. It is in this moment of hunger that the enemy began to "suggest a solution" to Jesus's problem. The enemy said to Him, "If you are the Son of God, turn these stones to bread." The enemy fires suggestive rounds with the stealth of a silencer. At times, it can be difficult to recognize that you are even being attacked because the suggestions made by the enemy always appear to have your best interest in mind, a means to an end, and a solution to your problem. Jesus's humanity was being tested at the highest level, and we know it to be so because this would not have been temptation if in His mind, He did not want it! How does Jesus handle this sniper round coming at Him in the form of a supply for His need?

If you will notice, Jesus did exactly what 2 Corinthians 10: 3-5 instructs us to do:

1. He does not enlist the flesh to fight a spiritual battle.

2. He allows the Holy Spirit to pull down the stronghold.

3. He takes responsibility for His part in the process by taking every thought in His head captive that went against the Word of God.

4. He lined what He "heard in His head" up with what "He knew in the Word."

Here is the harsh reality: you cannot take captive what goes against God's Word if you do not have God's Word in you! Jesus replied to the enemy's suggestion by saying,

"Man shall not live by bread alone, but every **Word** that proceeds out of the mouth of God." Do you have enough Word in you to compare the enemy's suggestions to? Even when the enemy attacks you with a variation of God's Word, do you have enough truth in you to recognize the lie?

CHAPTER 6
The Open Door Policy

I remember when I served in the military several years ago. My company commander wanted to build a good rapport with all the troops, so he put in place something called "the open door" policy. Basically, our commander was letting us know that his office would be "open" to the soldiers under his command because he wanted to encourage openness and transparency with the soldiers of that company. As inviting, sincere, and idealistic this policy was, my commander soon realized that **SOME DOORS HAD TO BE SHUT!** Unfortunately, many of us have unconsciously adopted an "open door" policy in our lives and are inviting things into our inner space unknowingly. Every day, we are going about life giving everything permission to enter our inner space because we are living by a policy that causes us to keep our doors open. Very seldom do people consider the amount of things they expose themselves to on a daily basis, and how what they have been exposed to influences their thinking.

Contrary to what we believe and may have been taught, **NOTHING** just appears in our minds. Every action comes from a thought, and every thought comes from somewhere. This is good news for you and me because it means since thoughts come from somewhere, we have the power to stop thoughts before they ever make it into our heads. If thoughts are coming from somewhere, we have the advantage; we just have to be able to recognize where those thoughts are coming from. As long as you allow yourself to believe that thoughts just appear randomly out of nowhere, you will continue to believe that you cannot do anything about them. I am convinced by the mere fact that you are reading this book that, in the words of the great Civil Rights Activist, Fannie Lou Hamer, "You are sick and tired of being sick and tired!" You have become exhausted, frustrated and done with what your thought life is doing to you, and you are ready to do something about it!

Gateways Into The Mind

Everything that happens within our thinking is introduced to our minds through what I will refer to as "gates". The different thought patterns that we have come to know as normal were developed from birth by different influences that entered our minds through "gates". You must understand that you were not born thinking the way you have been taught to think and process things. Parents, siblings, family, friends, culture, socioeconomic status, upbringings, geographical location and even television made significant contributions that ultimately shaped and developed the way we process our thoughts today. That is why it is so viably important for you to understand how you became the you that you are, so that you will know what about you needs to be fixed. You would be surprised at how much of a "lesser you" that you have embraced that was never intended to be part of your God-given makeup.

I like the word "gate" because it means an entrance into something, and gates suggest boundaries. In other words, where gates are, certain things are not and should not be welcomed in. If you do not come to terms with the fact that your mind has gates leading in and out of it, you will never see your mind for what it truly is: **PRIVATE PROPERTY!**

When the gates are not recognized, they cease to serve their purpose, which is to keep things that do not belong in your head out of your head. We must be very careful as to what we allow into our heads because it is much more difficult to get things out than it is to let things in. What took only one second to enter your mind may very well take an entire year, if you are fortunate, to get out of your mind. Let me explain. Have you ever heard the term: "Your mind is like sponge?" Well, it is true; it literally is! Think with me for a moment. If you were to spill a fruit punch drink on your counter-top and decided to clean up the mess with a sponge, after squeezing out the sticky red liquid from the sponge, the sponge will continue to hold the residue of what it soaked up! So it is with our "sponge-like" minds. Whatever we allow it to soak up, even though we squeeze it out, there is always a residue of what was soaked up that remains.

Consider the children of Israel in the Bible. Just as the sponge scenario indicated, they had been literally "squeezed out" of

Egyptian bondage, but the residue of Egypt had stained their minds. The residue from what they had soaked up in Egypt was so embedded into their thinking that the only way to fix it was to let them perish in the wilderness. God then brought their children into Canaan because they had not been contaminated by what their parents soaked up. What I am trying to say is your mind, if not detoxed, will only allow you to go but so far. An "old mind" will never be compatible with the "new place" God is trying to bring you to. We must come to realize that this mental stage upon which we fight is serious business and the most skilled of warriors understand that it is not about how many thoughts you can kick out of your head, but rather, not allowing contrary thoughts to enter your mind in the first place.

Let us briefly examine a few of these gates to give you an idea of how to recognize them in your own life.

The Eye Gate

The namesake of the book titled after him, Job declares that he has determined within himself to not allow his eyes the opportunity to cause him to sin. The NIV translation says it this way, "I made a covenant with my eyes not to look lustfully at a girl (Job 31:1)." Now, I understand that gazing upon a woman may not be *your* particular weakness. However, the principle of this text is relevant in any situation where you find your "eyes" letting images into your mind that eventually lead to counterproductive actions and behaviors. For example, how many times have you determined to cut back on spending until you saw that sale? You may have even mustered up the fortitude to leave the store, but found your way back a few days later because you just could not get that sale out of your mind! This is just one common example, but believe me, the list goes on and on. If you are anything like me, you are a visual person. You see and notice things around you. There is no harm in "looking" as long as you understand that what you see ultimately feeds your thought life, and your thoughts influence your actions and behaviors.

Many of us do not walk in the revelation Job had concerning what we give our eyes permission to see. Job understood that his eyes were, in fact, gates. Not only were his eyes instruments that allowed things in, but his eyes were also instruments that had the ability to keep unwanted things out. Job understood that he was the gatekeeper of his own mind and what he allowed himself to see or not see had everything to do with what his mind thought. In whatever context we put it, "looking" is not just looking. When we see things, our eyes photocopy and then plaster the image onto our minds. In Job's case, he understood that if he was careless with his eyes, he may have simply looked upon a woman at the marketplace, but that woman he looked at would have left an image in his mind. Although the woman was not physically present with him, the fact that he still has her image in his mind, means that he now has the ability to do a whole lot more with her in his head than he would ever dare to do with her in public. The principle of what Job is saying applies to every scenario where the eyes are concerned. Most of us are of the persuasion that "looking" is not a bad thing as long as we don't buy that item, touch that person, or go into that place. Nevertheless, "looking" is like the gateway drug that will always lead to an insatiable addiction. Once what you see gets into your head, you will begin to rationalize actions and behaviors that you had initially determined within yourself you would not partake of.

Adam and Eve have become cautionary tales of what can happen when we allow what we see to get into our heads. In Genesis, chapter 3, the serpent approached Eve and suggested to her that God had not said to her and Adam that they couldn't eat from the Tree of the Knowledge of Good and Evil. The NIV translation says, "Did God really say, 'You must not eat from any tree in the garden'? (Genesis 3:1)." What we overlook in this narrative is the fact that Eve must have already been "looking" at this forbidden tree; otherwise, the serpent would have never approached her with this temptation. In 1 Peter 5:8, the Bible describes the lion-like nature of the serpent. The scriptures tell us that he walks about looking for weaknesses in his victims that they may become EASY prey. All too often, we give the enemy credit for overthrowing us when, in many cases, we made ourselves EASY prey by exposing our weaknesses through what he has observed us "looking" at! The image of the fruit Eve was told not to partake of had become so embedded in her mind that she began to rationalize whether eating from the tree was right or wrong. Images that should have never entered your mind will begin to skew your judgment and cause you to justify behaviors and actions that you previously would have shunned. I know you are strong and you believe you are in absolute control of what you do and when you do it, but believe me, EVERY superhero has a kryptonite! Let us all become students of Eve's folly and begin to walk in the revelation of Job: "I made a covenant with MY eyes not to look lustfully at _____ **(fill in the blank)**."

Ear Gate

The Book of Proverbs is, for the most part, a collection of wise sayings popularly known and repeated amongst mankind. These stories express a truth based on common sense or the practical experiences of humanity. In the 4th Chapter of Proverbs in the 23rd verse, King Solomon exhorts us to guard our hearts (heart and mind is used interchangeably in this text) above all else that we guard. He says we must guard our hearts above all else because our inner life is the wellspring of our lives. In other words, we must be very careful as to what we allow inside of us because every part of our being drinks from our hearts. We do not want any part of our being drinking poisoned water. What is most interesting to me is that after King Solomon told us the importance of guarding our hearts, he went on to say, "Put away from you a **froward mouth**, and **perverse lips** put far from you (Proverbs 4:24 KJV)." The interpretation is twofold: First, the writer is addressing the communication that comes out of your own mouth, but just as important, the communication you allow yourself to hear out of other people's mouths. I want to focus on what we allow ourselves to hear from other people because quite frankly, what we say out of our own mouths is usually a byproduct of what we have heard others around us saying.

The "ear gate" is just as dangerous as the "eye gate" in that you cannot stop seeing just as you cannot stop hearing. We do not have the luxury of meandering through life independent of two of the most necessary senses we need to lead functional and productive lives. In a perfect world, it would be nice to have an on/off switch that could conveniently alleviate the unwanted challenges of these troublesome portals to the mind, but since this is not the case, we have the option of filtering what we give or what we deny access to our minds. God has made you the steward of your life, and as your own manager, YOU have the authority to hire or fire what influences your life. So, in essence, YOU and I get to determine the quality of our own lives based upon what type of wellsprings we allow our minds to drink from. And yes, what you allow yourself to hear in your life will determine that outcome.

      The writer warns us primarily of two types of communication that we must arduously protect our "waters" (mind) from. Let us examine the first: **A Froward Mouth**. A froward mouth can be defined as communication that is habitually disposed to disobedience and opposition to what is right. A perfect example of this at work would be again, Eve's interaction with the serpent in the Garden of Eden. Eve had already set herself up for a fall by gazing upon something that should have never been in her line of view. Genesis 3 records that there was a fairly long dialogue between her and the serpent BEFORE she eventually succumbed to what she saw and what she heard. One thing we oftentimes forget is that in spite of how wonderful our titles may be, how respected we are, how long we have been saved, and how good we have been lately, we are prone to do the wrong thing because our fallen nature cohabitates with us daily. On your best day, there are two of you living in that one body uncomfortably fighting for dominion. Your flesh (old man) and your spirit (new man) are always ready to answer, depending on which one is spoken to. You have to make sure that what you are hearing is addressing the right *you*. Because we were "shaped in iniquity" and "conceived in sin", according to Psalm 51:5, we cannot afford to expose our "ear gates" to communication that is compatible with our fallen, and sometimes, most dominant nature. As it was with Eve in humanity's most pristine state, if you hear wrong, you will eventually do wrong, and your life will go wrong because the wellspring that it drinks from has become contaminated. Another good Proverb says that your life will follow your head. Proverbs 23:7 reads, "As a man thinks within himself, so is he (NASB)." Ultimately, your life is a byproduct of your thought life and your thought life is a byproduct of what comes into your head through your gates.

Perverse Lips

Now, let us take a look at the second form of communication we must guard against: **perverse lips**. "Put far from you!" Proverbs 4:24 reads, "Put away from you a deceitful mouth, and perverse lips put far from you." Perverse lips can be described as any communication that speaks contrary to the Word of God in your life. This particular form of speech strikes a chord with me personally, because I can admit to giving away years of my life by allowing what other people said negatively or incorrectly about me to affect what I thought in my heart about myself. If you will notice, this particular form of communication, according to Proverbs 4:24, must be put "far from you." The challenge we will all face eventually, if we are to keep our "waters" clean and our thought life healthy is: **TO REMOVE "PERVERTED LIPS", WE MAY HAVE TO REMOVE THE PEOPLE THAT THE PERVERTED LIPS BELONG TO!** Perverted lips are dangerous, because in most cases, the people that those perverted lips belong to are close to you. For example, you will find that those closest to you will say the most negative things to you because they "knew you" so well at one stage of your life. Because of this, they are having a hard time dealing with the fact that the you that they "knew" so well is no longer at the place they are trying to find you.

I am reminded of Luke 24:1-6 when the two Marys went to the tomb where Jesus was laid to rest and the Angel asked them, "Why seek ye the living amongst the

dead? He is not here (KJV)." Just what the
two Marys attempted to do in the
referenced scripture, many of the people
we know attempt to do in our lives. They
run back to the place they saw us last and
find empty tombs! Initially, people in your
life will have the same reaction that the two
Marys did, which is to get into their feelings
of what they think should be and should not
be. It took a revelation carried by the
Angels from Heaven to get the point across
that Jesus was not at the place the grieving
Marys had last seen Him or the place they
thought they should find Him. It will also
take a revelation from God for the people
who "knew you" to find that you are not at
the place they last saw you or the place
they thought they should find you. Read this
very carefully: *Until God gives people a*
revelation of what He is doing in YOUR life,
YOU may have to put them "far" from you!
It is our nature to speak evil or negatively of
the things we cannot understand, but it is

also our choice as to whether or not we give audience to the negative things being spoken.

The opposite of negative is positive. You would be surprised at how positive your thinking will become as a result of eliminating "perverted lips" from your life. Please do not misunderstand me here. Constructive criticism, wise Godly counsel from trusted proven sources and healthy accountability should always be welcomed, and may, at times, feel negative, but they will always yield positive fruit. What we must guard ourselves against is the unlearned critique from people who have made themselves certified experts of us and our lives, but have no compass for their own lives! Such individuals will speak incorrectly concerning you EVERYTIME. A person cannot speak correctly about you or to anyone else if they do not have a correct point of reference to base their opinions on.

I would be remiss to not acknowledge the fact that it is neither your assignment nor mine to demonize those with "perverted lips", especially if we choose to keep them so close that we can hear them speak. In this case, we are just as guilty as they are.

REFLECTIONS

*What are some ways that you will begin
to guard your inner life?

_____

_____

_____

_____

_____

_____

*Identify some of the people in your life
that negatively influence you through their
negative communication.

_____

_____

_____

_____

_____

_____

*What part of your being has been drinking from "poisoned" waters, and what will you do to purify the well?

_____

_____

_____

_____

_____

_____

*As a result of what I have learned about the importance of "gates", from this day forward, I:

_____

_____

_____

_____

_____

_____

CHAPTER 7

Peace Given or Peace Received?

Is it peace given or peace received? What a remarkable question! As for me, I tend to succumb to the temptation of responding quickly to questions that require a great deal of study, consideration, and self-examination. Those things that we have heard often or perhaps believe we have great understanding of are the things we tend to take for granted and very seldom "check" ourselves out to ensure we are in fact walking in agreement with.

The definition of peace, according to *Merriam-Webster Dictionary*, is: "Freedom from disquieting or oppressive thoughts or emotions." The peace that God gives us brings about an inner stability that is reflected tangibly in our lives, because whatever your inner life is, your outer life will be. With that being said, it becomes imperative that we guard our inner spaces at all costs! We must come to understand that our minds become most vulnerable when we abandon our God-given peace to pursue matters that we do not and cannot understand. Jesus told His disciples in the Gospel of St. John 14:27, "Peace I leave with you; my peace I give you (NIV)." That statement implies that Jesus left His peace in our care and under our watch so, we are to be good stewards over that which He left to our care.

It is very important that we do not confuse His peace with our peace because there is a peace that we can **man**ufacture (man-made) as a substitute for the real thing. The counterfeit, or as I like to call it, **man**ufactured peace, will always be characterized by a peace that is predicated upon "outer" circumstances. For example, how many times have you professed to have peace as a result of how wonderful things were at the moment, or perhaps, how well your day went at the job? What you were experiencing, beloved, is "**man**ufactured" peace. We have all experienced manufactured peace, and in many cases, we've manufactured peace for ourselves and others. You found peace in something rather than allowing the peace that God has given to be found in you. The peace we normally experience comes as the result of what the present moment is giving us and how wonderful we feel because of it. In essence, what we have come to celebrate as God-given peace is nothing more than outer stimuli; a peace produced by the conditions that surround us at the time.

When authentic, God-given peace is at work, there is freedom from mental, emotional, and oppressive turmoil regardless of what is or is not happening around you. How is this even possible, you may ask? Very simply put, God-given peace is what happens inside of you that is totally independent of outer stimuli. God produced peace does not need the aid of a good moment to liberate you; in fact, real peace is not defined by how peaceful things are around you, but rather, your ability to keep a peaceful disposition on the inside when everything on the outside is completely out of control. Having pastored for over 13 years internationally and domestically, it is safe to say that I have had the opportunity to minister and interact with just about every type of person there is. One thing I have discovered about human nature is that we all have a tendency to be a little bit delusional concerning our perception of ourselves. We have a proclivity of seeing ourselves from the perspective of who we want to be, rather than seeing ourselves as we truly are. To get someone to entertain the possibility that they may be operating in a "**man**ufactured" peace is one of the hardest things to do. Maybe you failed to recognize some of these characteristics of the counterfeit playing out in your life, so I ask you this question before we proceed: **"Do you struggle with taking on the nature of your circumstances?"**

The God Of Peace And The Peace Of God

The Bible informs us in Philippians 4:7 that there is a "peace that surpasses all understanding (KJV)". In other words, our Father in Heaven equips us with a peace that settles our mind, thoughts, and emotions... even in situations where we do not have the ability to understand all we may be experiencing or all that may be happening in our lives. No other peace other than the peace of God has the ability to keep your mind at bay while you matriculate through seasons of uncertainty. The dark influences and powers of the enemy thrive and live in chaos and confusion. When we abandon the safety and surety of God's peace for an imitation, we soon find that what we sought to find refuge in, quickly comes down upon our "heads"... literally (pun intended). When we attempt to understand things where understanding has not been given, the result is confusion and chaos. There are some things God will not explain, because to truly understand them, you may have to experience them first. Peace allows you to go through what you do not understand without trying to force an explanation. Over the course of my life, I have learned that when taking a test of any kind, whether natural or spiritual, a teacher saying too much can be worse than a teacher saying too little!

At times, I am willing to admit that I had been hoping to stumble upon some great revelatory instruction as to appropriating this peace that Jesus said He has already given me. That sounds like most of us, right? How many times have you prayed for God to "peace you together" and it seemed as though peace had started a game of hide and seek and forgot to tell you that you were it? There is a reason peace seems so elusive to most of us, even though Jesus delivered the package to our door before we ever had a door to deliver it to. You see, no matter how much we pray, ask or even beg, Jesus cannot do again what He has already done! He already told us that He left *His* peace with us (past tense). Asking God for more peace is like children asking for more food when they have not eaten what is already on their plate! The begging children may feel ignored, but in reality, it is the children that have ignored what has already been placed in front of them.

Isaiah 26:3 gives us a very simple and pragmatic way to appropriate the peace we have been given. Isaiah basically tells us that *if* we keep our minds on God, He, in return, will keep us in perfect peace. Perfect peace is a mature "God kind" of peace that steadies our mind on God (who He is and His attributes), not on what He is doing. In essence, keep your mind on the One who gave you peace and the peace He gave you will keep you.

When we abandon the peace that God has given us by recklessly pursuing matters that He has not given us revelation or understanding of, we are, in fact, authorizing our finite minds to try and figure out infinite things. When the mind runs into a dead end, the natural reaction is to worry, and worry opens the door to oppressive thoughts and emotions that lead us into other things that make us easy prey for the enemy. Many of us have adapted to this type of thinking, all the while claiming to have peace.

Our adversary the Devil, does not want us to live out our lives from a place of inner peace because peace puts everything in proper perspective. You are better able to see things as they truly are, without the temptation of allowing your mind to run down every rabbit trail presented to you, through the skewed perspective of an unguarded moment. Peace places you in a responsive mode versus a reactive mode, while creating an environment that exposes the enemy's attacks against your mind. Where and when are you most likely to recognize that you are potentially in harm's way? Would it be in a large crowd where everyone is talking and moving about, or in a clear and controlled environment where things are not as ungoverned? In this survey, most of us would choose the clear and controlled environment. It is a no-brainer, right? Well, that is the contribution that peace makes to every environment or situation it is given permission to exist in. Peace quiets the noise, dissipates the crowd and creates an environment that is conducive to having a clear head. Isaiah 26:3 makes it very clear: "If you keep peace, peace will keep you!"

I began this chapter with the words of Jesus recorded in John's Gospel 14:27. Jesus said, "Peace I leave with you, **my** peace I give unto you." If Jesus has given us His peace, it is up to you and me to keep the peace He gave us without creating substitutions for it, even though keeping it may seem too difficult a task at times. What makes counterfeits so tempting is the fact that to obtain the real thing costs too much, but when you consider how quickly the imitation fails to deliver on what it promised you, you end up paying twice as much for the real thing you could have gotten the first time.

I can remember, on multiple occasions, sitting down in my soft recliner with a hot cup of tea or coffee and getting my last few thoughts together before heading to church to minister. During those times, I found myself thinking, "The peace of God is all over me!" The Lord allowed me to persevere in that ideology for years before finally stepping in and lovingly whispering these words to me: "That is not My peace you feel; you are feeling the effects of the caffeine in your beverage." Wow...talk about letting the air out of the balloon. Like many of us often respond to soft rebuke, my heart sank until I realized God's bigger objective for chiming in on what I thought was a "peace-filled moment". You see, I realized that in God's love and desire for me to experience the best He had for me, I first had to be released from "my version" of what I thought His best was. Substitutions, in any form, are NOT the real thing, even if they do give off some effects of the real thing.

This simple encounter I had with the Holy Spirit revolutionized my life on many levels. I began to realize that the enemy counts on us to over spiritualize EVERYTHING, because by doing so, we often credit God for doing less when He is capable of doing so much more! For example, if I'd continued to believe that God was responsible for the "peace" I felt when I sat down with my beverage of choice, I would have resigned myself to the belief that peace is not available on that level *unless* I sat down with a cup of coffee. Consider how many times you thought within yourself, "I sure can't wait until I can finish _____ and indulge in _____." Why do you have to finish **whatever** you're doing before you can enjoy the peace of God? Why are you not able to experience the peace of God **while** you are engaged in whatever it is you are doing?

I have found that those who over spiritualize EVERYTHING, have a tendency of getting so deep that they venture off into waters without a life jacket, and subsequently end up drowning in their OWN depth! When God's peace is in operation, you cannot vacillate in and out of it like the pendulum on my vintage German clock. The pendulum on my clock swings back and forth, never in one place for long because its movements are predicated by the time. The fact that you are IN peace will not allow you to come OUT of it because of what may be happening at that time. This may seem unrealistic for many of us, simply because we have grown accustomed to peace that does not keep us stable if the time is not right! Dear friend, I dare you to believe that God's peace is able to keep you as secure and stable as it did Jesus when it allowed Him to sleep undisturbed in the lower parts of a boat while in the middle of a typhoon (see Matthew 8:23-27).

The peace of God allows us to rest undisturbed in the God of peace. This peace is a type of Sabbath rest for the New Testament believer and it allows us to cease from our own labors and turmoil, and trust God to be the supplier for all of our needs. Many of us are too tired to get much of anything done for the Kingdom because we are too easily awakened from our rest and forced to try and handle the things we worry about but can do nothing about. Let's have a human moment and consider how we feel when we are awakened from our sleep too soon. Okay, you get my point! When we do not get the rest we need in the natural, we do not function as efficiently as we do when we are well rested. With little to no rest, we are quick to become agitated. Just as it is in the natural realm, so it is in the realm of the spirit.

God has provided a "safe house" for us that will hide us from the **effects** of the things that befall us in life. He never promised that things would not go wrong or unexpected, but He did promise that in spite of our tribulations, we would have peace in Him (see John 16:33). Psalm 91:1 declares, "He that dwelleth in the **secret place** of the most High shall abide under the shadow of the Almighty." Peace provides a "secret place" that does not allow the *effects* of trouble, chaos and turmoil to find you! The only way these distractions can find you in the "secret place" is if YOU choose to come out and expose yourself. I assure you, beloved, that once you have given yourself permission to experience the "secret place", coming OUT of it will no longer be an option for you. My prayer today is that we may all find the courage and fortitude to enter that "secret place" and remain!

REFLECTIONS

*In what ways have you created
substitutions for real peace?

_____

_____

_____

_____

_____

_____

*In what ways will you adjust your prayers
so that your prayers do not become the
hindrance to appropriating the peace of
God in your life?

_____

_____

_____

_____

_____

_____

*Identify some things that have a tendency to "awaken" you from your rest in God.

_____

_____

_____

_____

_____

_____

*How will you respond to these distractions from this point on?

_____

_____

_____

_____

_____

_____

CONCLUSION OF THE MATTER

We operate most effectively when we are thinking, living, and behaving out of the mind of Christ, the very mind that we received when we were born again. In order to operate in the mind of Christ, we must first decide that our current unregenerate minds are inadequate to perform at the level for which we were designed to function. We must also decide that the majority of our frustrations are rooted in our unwillingness to change our mindsets. Then, we must be willing to abandon ideologies, theologies, philosophies and traditions that are no longer compatible with where we currently are and plan to go in our lives. The Bible calls this process the "renewing of the mind." We decide the quality of our thought life based upon the type of information we allow into our heads. You have been made a steward of your mind, so however you manage it, will dictate how your thoughts manage your life!

www.ingramcontent.com/pod-product-compliance
Lightning Source LLC
Chambersburg PA
CBHW060953040426
42445CB00011B/1141